D1441196

Levi Coffin, Quaker

Breaking the Bonds of Slavery
in Ohio and Indiana

By Mary Ann Yannessa

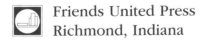

Friends United Press
Richmond, Indiana

Cover design by Shari Pickett Veach

Cover photo: Levi Coffin. Used by permission of Janice McGuire, Levi Coffin House, Fountain City, Indiana.

Library of Congress Cataloging-in-Publication Data

Yannessa, Mary Ann, 1935-
    Levi Coffin : Quaker breaking the bonds of slavery in Ohio and
    Indiana / Mary Ann Yannessa.
        p. cm.
    Includes bibliographical references (p.).
    ISBN 0-944350-54-2
    1. Coffin, Levi, 1798-1877. 2. Abolitionists--United States--Biogra-
phy. 3. Quakers--United States--Biography 4. Antislavery movements--
Ohio--Cincinnati--History--19th century. 5. Cincinnati (Ohio)--Race
relations. 6. Antislavery movements--Ohio--History--19th century. 7.
Antislavery movements--Indiana--History--19th century. 8. Underground railroad--Ohio. 9. Underground railroad--Indiana. I. Title.

E450.C65 Y36 2001
973.7'115'092--dc21
[B]

                                                        2001023837

Dedicated, with love,
to my husband Charlie,
my "light within."

and to my sons and daughters-in-law
who "light up my life."

Special thanks to all those members of the Religious Society
of Friends, as well as others of nineteenth-century America,
who never ceased to believe that slavery was wrong,
and were willing to do something about it.

Contents

"If you come to us, and are hungry, we will feed you; if thirsty, we will give you drink, if naked, we will clothe you; if sick, we will minister to your necessities; if in prison, we will visit you; if you need a hiding place from pursuers, we will provide one that even bloodhounds will not scent out."

—Credo of the American Anti-Slavery Society

Prologue

There existed, side by side, in the first half of the nineteenth century, a faith, a movement and a man. That faith was that of the Religious Society of Friends, the movement was abolitionism, and the man was Levi Coffin. Within America, the institution of slavery had existed since the early 1600s. It had wrapped the citizens of the cities, the farms, the plantations, in its snakelike grip and was squeezing the lifeblood out of both the victims and the perpetrators. It had such power and it had such viciousness. This social and economic structure led to a movement known as abolitionism. Out of the abolition movement grew the beginnings of the Underground Railroad.

Today nearly everyone is familiar with the term Underground Railroad. There are two reasons why the Underground Railroad existed in America. Firstly, it existed because wealthy white property owners held persons of color against their will. These white owners valued their black slaves as property and in most cases treated them as less than human. Ultimately these captive and courageous men and women sought their freedom by escaping their pursuers and following the North Star toward the Promised Land. Their escape routes were hidden and secret, almost mysteriously "underground." Secondly, the Underground Railroad existed because of men and women who challenged conformity and dared to speak out against the injustice of slavery. Levi Coffin was one such man. His Quaker faith was his life. Because of this faith and his belief in the power of one person's life for good, he influenced a movement and a country.

Coffin did the majority of his work for the release and relief of the African American slaves in Ohio and Indiana. Emboldened by the faith of his ancestors, he put his life on the line to validate what he deemed to be God's directive to him, that of "do[ing] to others as you would have them do to you" (Matthew 7:12). The abolitionist movement and Coffin's subsequent Underground Railroad activity became his identity. Did the time make the man? Perhaps so, but Levi Coffin did not shrink from his times. He walked through his life with little concern for himself. An ordinary man with ordinary foibles, a sense of humor, and a flair for the dramatic, he was sincere in his unflinching desire to rid the country of the fleshdealers. He worked continuously to free the men, women, and children who lived within the boundaries of slavery. He did all he could, especially in Ohio and Indiana, to bring the institution down. The demise of the slavery machine depended on many outstanding men and women devoted to a cause. No finer example of this devotion can be seen than that of the Quaker gentleman in his Quaker garb: Levi Coffin.

LEVI COFFIN, QUAKER

New Garden, North Carolina (1798-1819) 1

L evi Coffin's spiritual heritage and roots, as a member of the
Religious Society of Friends, were in England. His father was
a Quaker farmer who had originally emigrated from the New
England island of Nantucket. Levi Coffin was born in the year 1798 in
New Garden, North Carolina and was named after his father. While
the younger Levi was brought up to be a farmer and a good Quaker
like his father, he was anything but isolated from society. The stereo-
typical picture of a Quaker—somber, plain, and pious—is simply that:
an oversimplified view of Quakers as a group.

Founded by George Fox, who was born in 1624 in Leicestershire,
England, the Religious Society of Friends proclaimed the equality of
persons and the "inner light" available to a Christ-filled individual no
matter what color, sex, or creed. But these men and women of
England, even in the 1600s, lived in the world; they worked and were
a part of society. Judith Jennings quotes D. B. Davies, in his book,
The Problem of Slavery in Western Culture, as saying "the Society of
Friends had a 'gift for pragmatic adjustment'... which allowed them to
survive when other sectarian groups of the seventeenth century
failed" (Jennings 1977, 30).

So, too, the members of the Religious Society of Friends who
emigrated from England to the shores of America were a part of
mainstream eighteenth-century colonial society. They were not an

isolated group, whose beliefs in the equality of all humans before God and in nonviolence *mandated* acceptance of abolitionism. Abolitionism was not an easy choice for many Quakers. The Religious Society of Friends in North America were often substantial slave-holders, who had to face a difficult decision between giving up a valuable source of labor or resisting the abolitionist members of their society and continuing to hold slaves (Soderlund 1985, 5). Values had to change, and the moral rectitude of preachers and the persistence of the members of the Religious Society of Friends had to prevail.

In the 1700s a new voice arose among North American Quakers. John Woolman, born in 1720 in New Jersey, less than twenty miles from Philadelphia, emphasized the original religious conviction of George Fox. In 1754, Woolman composed a strong antislavery letter to all Quaker groups in Pennsylvania and New Jersey titled "Some Considerations on the Keeping of Negroes." This letter was largely responsible for the advancement of the antislavery sentiment at the Philadelphia Yearly Meeting of 1755 (Moulton 1971, 12). It was also influential in condemning the slave trade at London Yearly Meeting in June 1758. At Woolman's insistence, the Religious Society of Friends adopted a formal statement urging their fellow members to free their slaves, arranging for visitation of slaveholders, and decreeing that anyone who bought and sold slaves was to be excluded from partici-pating in the business affairs of the Yearly Meeting (Moulton 1971, 13). In 1762, "Considerations on the Keeping of Negroes Part Second," an even stronger declamation against slavery, was published.

John Woolman himself, in 1757, had written a letter to the New Garden, North Carolina Friends community. He reminded his brothers and sisters that "where slaves are purchased to do our labour, numerous difficulties attend it...I have been informed that there are a large number of Friends in your parts who have no slaves and in tender and most affectionate love I now beseech you to keep clear from purchasing any" (Moulton 1971, 67-69). In 1767 Woolman mentions visiting New Garden Week Day Meeting. His admonitions and cautions on the slavery questions were of greatest import. It can be surmised that his personal visitations to individual Quakers included many in New Garden, North Carolina.

"...I have been informed that there are a large number of Friends in your parts who have no slaves...," wrote John Woolman. Some of those numbers to whom he refers had to have been the Coffin family. Levi Coffin directly inherited his antislavery principles. His parents and grandparents were opposed to slavery and no one on either side of the family ever owned slaves. His cousin, Vestal Coffin, is today often cited as the organizer, in 1819, of the Underground Railroad in North Carolina, near what is today, Guilford College. Addison Coffin, Vestal's son, entered its service in early youth and became known as one of its conductors.

As a child, Coffin continually endured the sight of white owners abusing their black slaves. Frequently he saw gangs handcuffed and chained together, being led along the roadside toward their eventual sale to plantation owners further south. He dates his own personal conversion to abolitionism to an incident that occurred when he was only seven. He was with his father, who was chopping wood, when one such gang approached them. His father spoke to them, asking them why they were chained and being led away. The reply was that they were chained so that they would not make their escape and return to their wives and children. It was inconceivable to Levi that his father should ever be taken away from him, and that incident awakened, even at so young an age, the sympathy with the oppressed and the hatred of oppression and injustice of every kind, "which were the motives that influenced my whole after-life" (Coffin 1898, 12-13).

By the time Levi was fifteen, he and his cousin Vestal had frequently helped slaves on their way North. Runaways knew they were temporarily safe if they found shelter in the fields surrounding the Coffin farm. As Levi went out to feed the hogs, he would wander to where the slaves were gathered and give them food from his own meal. Coffin was already warning slaves when their capture was imminent or finding households that would agree to hide a slave until safety was assured. He was not always successful, but he developed discipline and determination in these years along with Vestal Coffin and his own immediate family. He and Vestal, well respected members of their own New Garden Friends community, continued to aid escaping slaves, even though this work was never officially condoned by North Carolina Yearly Meeting. Individuals who participated in helping slaves escape were quite often disavowed by the Society, which, although it continued to speak out against the injustice of slavery and to forbid members to own slaves, decidedly did not condone interference with others who chose this manner of existence.

In the meantime, many Quakers both in Britain and the colonies (especially Philadelphia, where most lived) were already increasingly aware of the narrow interpretation of "doing unto others...." Some Friends did not accept John Woolman's directive because it had become far too easy to use African American labor for their own increased wealth. There were many others along the mid-Atlantic seaboard, however, who were learning that the slaves were indeed more than just property. They were humans, who could learn or refuse to learn, loved and raised families, obeyed respectfully or rebelled, and socialized with other blacks and whites. They stole food and money, committed suicide, ran away to be with their families, learned to read, and preached religion (Soderlund 1985, 78). These members of the Religious Society of Friends were beginning to sense that holding blacks as slaves was sinful because they were the equals of whites in all ways the eyes and heart could evidence. They were also beginning to realize that violence, which Quakers so abhorred, eventually would be the result of holding these blacks hostage. One hundred years before the Civil War, John Woolman prophesied in his *Journal*, "...The seeds of great calamity and desolation are sown and growing fast on this continent" (Moulton 1971, 7).

The antislavery movement, as weighty a problem as it was within the Religious Society of Friends, especially in North Carolina, was never a clearly defined movement of men and women going in the same direction to achieve the same goal. Those who proclaimed freedom for the slaves were idealists saddled with human foibles and fears. This humanness is one of the endearing qualities of Levi Coffin. Portraits show him as a strong, solemn individual, giving the impression of having a somewhat tall frame. No one describes him, however, except to say that he was a dedicated abolitionist and devout Quaker, whose first law was his conscience and the law of Jesus Christ. His personality shows in many of the stories related in his *Reminiscences* and in stories others tell of him, but no one draws an elaborate picture of Coffin as a particularly spiritual or super-human individual. His visage was no doubt of little concern to the thousands of suffering individuals who knew him by his deeds. We can suppose he was very much an ordinary man who acted in extraordinary ways to effect change.

From New Garden to Newport, Indiana (1819-1826) 2

"I was not converted to peace principles then, and I felt like fighting for the slave," Coffin said, when speaking of his active participation against slavery in the years before he turned twenty-one. His blood ran as red and hot as any young man's when confronted with danger and injustice. "Pulling one over" on the institution also played a big role in the excitement of the game. "The dictates of humanity came in opposition to the law of the land, and we ignored the law," said Coffin (Coffin 1898, 25).

The law of the land had, by this time, become more hostile to blacks seeking freedom. New laws had been formed to counter slave uprisings or to punish escaping slaves. In 1793, the First Fugitive Slave Act passed, authorizing any state in the Union, or territories northwest or south of the Ohio River, to return any person who had fled slavery. (See Appendix A.) In 1804, Ohio enacted the Black Laws, which prohibited the "Negro...to settle or reside in the state unless he first produced a certificate from some court attesting his freedom." (See Appendix B.)

More laws meant more work for Levi Coffin. This advanced stage of abolitionism necessitated more and more secrecy. Much had to be done at night, under cover of darkness, to circumvent the slavehunters. The rough outline of the Underground Railroad was taking shape in New Garden, as early as 1810, and Levi and Vestal

Coffin were already instruments in its formation.

The particular term "Underground Railroad," used in connection with the work of aiding the escaping slaves, seems not to have been used until almost 1831. One story is told about a slave named Tice Davids, who was escaping to Ohio. His master followed him to the Ohio River, where he literally disappeared. The master spent hours looking for him and is reported to have told his friends that "he must have gone off on an underground railroad" (Cosner 1991, 26). John Brown referred to the escape routes as "subterranean pass-ways" (Siebert 1898, 339). There are multiple incidences of escaping slaves who were reported to have vanished, only to have surfaced in a distant place, saved by men and women devoted to seeing these fugitives safely to a destination far removed from their captors. These captors became known as "bloodhounds." The workers on the way came to be known as "conductors" and "agents," places of safety were referred to as "stations" or "depots," forms of transportation for the slave get-aways were "locomotives," and the routes of escape were "tracks." There was, of course, no railroad, or tracks, at least at first. Swamps, fields, the cover of night, and wet banks of the rivers were the escape routes for the fugitives who ran toward freedom.

The Underground Railroad could authentically be called the first secret service agency in America (Wilbur H. Siebert 1898). Yet it is a subject known only in part. Its story has been pieced together from scraps of written information and oral accounts "after the fact," for its success lay only in its secrecy.

There never was just one Underground Railroad; the term re-ferred to a number of escape routes through the North as well as some that led South, specifically to the Seminole Nation in Florida, or to other countries. Along these routes a network of safe houses with sympathetic hosts who helped escaping slaves evolved. Slaves from the deep South—hundreds of miles from free soil—found escape far more difficult than their brothers and sisters further north. Pursued by slave catchers and hunting dogs, fugitive slaves in Georgia or Alabama were almost sure to be caught, savagely whipped, and in many cases, sold away from family and friends. These slaves of the deep south often used the southern escape routes into Indian territory, rather than trying the long trek through the infested swamps and bloodhound-baited backcountry further north. The fear the more northern slaves had of being sold further south often prompted many to start their journey of escape toward the Ohio River.

The runaway slave was neither passive nor helpless. There are many heroes of the abolitionist movement, one of the finest examples being Levi Coffin. Larry Gara, in his book *The Liberty Line*, has taken issue with the reader who paints the Underground Railroad workers, or abolitionists, as the *only* heroes in this 50-year struggle for freedom. We must not forget, Gara says, the slave who "panted for release from his chains" and started his or her escape journey, often through swamps, islands and forests, and often through the most dangerous part of the journey alone. (Gara 1961, 3).

In 1822, a convention of the Religious Society of Friends was held in New Garden, North Carolina. Its concern was, specifically, the question of emancipation of the African American. The American Colonization Society had been organized in 1817 for the purpose of sending freedmen back to Africa. It operated as an alternative to Emancipation. Over a thousand blacks went to the Free Republic of Liberia in Africa during the next decade. Quakers in North Carolina availed themselves of this means of helping slaves, when they could no longer send them North (Hesseltine 1936, 246). A passage from Levi Coffin's own publication, *Reminicences* reflects the increasingly difficult choices about the slavery issue, even within the Religious Society of Friends.

> ...Quite a number of slaveholders were present who favor gradual manumission and colonization. They argued that if the slaves were manumitted, they must be sent to Africa; it would not do for them to remain in this country; they must return to Africa, and this must be made a condition of their liberty...This produced a sharp debate. Many of us were opposed to making colonization a condition of freedom, believing it to be an odious plan of expatriation concocted by slaveholders, to open a drain by which they might get rid of negroes, and thus remain in more secure possession of their slave property. They considered free negroes a dangerous element among slaves. We had no objection to free negroes going to Africa of their own free will, but to compel them to go as a condition of freedom was a movement to which we were conscientiously opposed and against which we strongly contended (Coffin 1898, 75).

It was in the fall of that same year, 1822, that Coffin accompanied his brother-in-law, Benjamin White, and White's family to Indiana. North Carolina was becoming more and more repressive for those who opposed slavery, and Quakers by the thousands began to "remove" themselves to the North, particularly Indiana or Ohio, free states where, the Quakers reasoned, they could live their principles with fewer restrictions. In these states, under the Ordinance of 1787, neither slavery nor involuntary servitude, except as punishment of crime, was allowed. Dr. Stephen B. Weeks, in *Southern Quakers and Slavery*, writes: "It may be an open question as to how many of these particular emigrants would have gone west had there been no slavery in the South. But that slavery did have an overwhelming influence...no one can deny" (Weeks 1968, 291).

Thus, Coffin took a look at the West in 1822, at age twenty-four. He remained with the Whites about one year. While in Indiana he became increasingly more convinced that he and the rest of his family should leave New Garden permanently and follow the Whites to the Free States. It was evident to Coffin that slavery and Quakerism could not prosper together (Coffin 1898, 76). He returned to New Garden to find that his family and many of his friends were eager to return with him to Indiana, where they could be freer to practice their convictions.

On October 28, 1824, Levi Coffin and Catharine White, a longtime friend, were married in the Hopewell Meetinghouse in North Carolina. Catharine and Levi had grown up in the same neighborhood and had known each other from childhood. Catharine was then a member of the Hopewell Monthly Meeting, where her father had moved a few years before. Levi turned twenty-six on his wedding day and Catharine was twenty-one. There is every indication that from the beginning of their marriage they worked as a team for the release of the runaway slaves who sought their help. They had been farmers while they remained in New Garden and now intended to farm in Indiana. It was not long until they made their decision to move west,

11

where so many of their family and friends had already settled. Indiana held out hope of more freedom to believe and support the abolition movement. Levi's parents had already moved there in 1825. With their son, Jesse, the Coffins removed to Newport, Indiana (now Fountain City) in 1826.

Twenty Years in
Newport, Indiana (1826-1847)   3

N ine miles north of Richmond, Indiana, Newport (now
Fountain City) was just six miles from the Ohio state line. A
number of free African Americans, mostly from North
Carolina, had settled in the Newport area (Coffin 1898, 107). They
were descendents of slaves liberated by the Religious Society of
Friends many years before. Fugitive slaves began to take refuge with
these black families, but it was not long before they were pursued
and captured. As an option, the Coffins offered their home as a
shelter, and it soon became well known to the escapees that they
would find a welcome there.

The refugees were mostly from the border states of Virginia and
Kentucky, as well as from Tennessee. They crossed from Virginia or
Kentucky into Ohio, which had a boundary of nearly four hundred
miles along these two slave states, or they came from Kentucky into
Indiana and moved north across Lake Erie into Canada. From Tennes-
see fugitives went either by river or overland through Kentucky to the
Ohio River, where they crossed with the help of the abolitionists
(Blockson 1994, 72-73). Three principal lines from the South con-
verged at the Coffin house in Newport: one from Cincinnati, one from
Madison, Indiana and one from Jefferson, Indiana. (see Appendix C).
Freedom for the fugitive, of course, did not mean the Ohio River, or
Cincinnati, or Newport, Indiana. These were only stops on the way to

freedom, which meant, at least, Michigan, but primarily southern Canada. Slavery in Lower Canada had been outlawed in 1800.

Coffin's *Reminiscences* do not record much about his personal family life. He had a wife, growing children, a large house, and certainly animals to feed and care for. Soon Levi pursued business opportunities to add to the often scanty and undependable income of farming. It was not long after he moved to Newport, Indiana that he started a mercantile business. In 1836, after ten years, he built an oil mill and began to manufacture linseed oil. His business did not always prosper, for there were those people who were vehemently opposed to his activity with escaping slaves. When times were slack and business falling off, though, it seemed that new customers came to take the place of those who left. He tells us in *Reminiscences* that:

> ...for a while my business prospects were discouraging, yet my faith was not shaken, nor my efforts for the slaves lessened. New settlements were filling up with emigrants from North Carolina and other States. My trade increased, and I enlarged my business...The Underground Railroad business increased as time advanced, and it was attended with heavy expenses, which I could not have borne had not my affairs been prosperous. I found it necessary to keep a team and a wagon always at command, to convey the fugitive slaves on their journey...Sometimes, when we had large companies, one or two other teams and wagons were required" (Coffin 1898, 110-111).

The artist, Charles T. Webber, in 1893, depicted this scene in his famous painting, which now hangs in the Cincinnati Art Museum. It has been reproduced in many books on the Underground Railroad.

In spite of, or perhaps because of, his intensely involved life, Coffin was elected a director of the Richmond branch of the State Bank, which played a big role in keeping pro-slavery men in check. His associations with businessmen and his popularity with everyone because of his genuineness and good humor gave him an advantage when helping the fleeing slave. He was an energetic, enthusiastic member of the Indiana Yearly Meeting of Friends and on the Committee on the Concerns of the People of Color. He had taught for a while in North Carolina before moving to Indiana, and he continued to remain interested in education for the children of the free blacks all his life. Through the Committee on the Concerns of the People of Color, he encouraged education for the children of any free African American who were within reach of the Indiana Yearly Meeting. Because of his interest in education, he opened an antislavery library in Newport, where he set up a depository of antislavery publications (Coffin 1898, 224).

By 1844, Coffin had become convinced that it was wrong to sell, buy or use any product of slave labor, and he began to renew his search for groceries and cotton goods that were the sole result of free labor. He investigated the possibility of opening a Free Store in Newport that would only carry merchandise supplied by free labor. He found some associations existing in Philadelphia and New York, which manufactured goods of free-labor cotton and imported sugar and other supplies from the British West Indies and other localities where slavery did not exist. He managed to buy a limited stock for his Newport store and sold it to abolitionists at a very small profit compared to what he might have made from slave-produced goods.

John Woolman had originated this broad idea of the Free Produce Movement. As far back as 1757, at a yearly meeting in Virginia, the question was asked, "Are any concerned in buying or vending goods unlawfully imported, or prize goods?" John Woolman observed that Quaker principles opposed "purchasing any merchandise taken by the sword." His premise was that the taking of Negroes was by no other method (Rosenblatt 1969, 45). He argued that the use of goods produced by slave labor was as bad as slaveholding itself. It caused the continuation of slavery through the inducement for the slaveholder to continue to hold his slave in bondage to maintain an economic advantage. "The receiver of stolen goods is as bad as the thief," John Woolman repeated over and over again, and the Quakers as a group generally supported his sentiment (Nuermberger 1942, 4).

The first real organization to advance the idea of boycotting slave labor goods was probably the one founded in Wilmington, Delaware, in 1826 (Nuermberger 1942, 13). The idea was rapidly promulgated at Quaker meetings, and in that same year it was being spread in Ohio. At first Coffin had a problem with the idealism of the cause versus the reality of the cost of the items. He wrote to the American Free Produce Association from Newport:

> ...we have many difficulties to contend with,...the great difference in the price of the goods and the poorness of the assortment stile...are great barriers in the way. The people cannot understand why there should be so much difference in the cost...If Free goods can be brought down about on a level with other goods a great many may be sold in the west (Nuermberger 1942, 64).

Meanwhile, all was not well for the Coffins within their own branch of the Religious Society of Friends. There were Quakers in the Indiana Yearly Meeting who did not sanction their continued activity with the Underground Railroad. A number of members wanted Quakers to take a less active role in the freeing of the slaves. Some still favored colonization or gradual emancipation (Coffin 1898, 230). In 1842 yearly meetings had advised members not to unite in abolition societies, nor to open meetinghouses for abolition meetings. The atmosphere became so antagonistic to abolition that it led to a separation in the Indiana Yearly Meeting of Friends. In 1843 Coffin and his family had been disowned for their antislavery activity. With other abolitionists he formed a separate Yearly Meeting of Antislavery Friends that same year (Coffin 1898, 232). Later when antislavery sentiment increased and more and more Northerners came forward to join the abolitionist cause, there was a reuniting of the two factions (Coffin 1898, 233, 246). From his early days in New Garden, North Carolina until his death, Levi Coffin never put the law of the land or even the caution of his beloved Religious Society of Friends above his conscience.

This departure from Indiana Yearly Meeting may have acted as a catalyst in Coffin's decision to move his family to Cincinnati, where Abolitionist friends were asking him to establish a Free Store. In 1846, Coffin wrote again to Samuel Rhodes of the American Free Produce Association saying, "...he (Dr. Thacker from Yalobusha County, Mississippi) pays his slaves for Their Labor, gives them a part of the cotton they raise, he has a Cotton Gin, will raise about 20 bales...there can be, he thinks about 150 bales of Free Cotton got in the neighborhood" (Nuermberger 1942, 70). The members of the

Salem Free Produce Association Meeting that same year chose Coffin to be the person to open the wholesale Free Produce Store in Cincinnati. Cincinnati was the city which best suited the reorganization of the Western Free Produce Association. Coffin declined at first, due to both financial and personal reasons, but no one else qualified. Despite his misgivings, he succumbed to the urgings of associates, rented his house in Newport, and moved to Cincinnati April 22, 1847. He planned on staying only five years.

Levi and Catharine felt a real separation on leaving Newport, Indiana. It had been their home for twenty years. In his *Reminiscences* he reflects that he

> ...had lived in Newport twenty years, and was much
> attached to my house and to my friends and acquaintances
> there. A few years before I had built a dwelling house,
> taking much pains to make it comfortable and convenient
> in all its appointments, with the expectation of occupying
> it as long as I lived. Neither I or my wife thought that we
> would like city life...(Coffin 1898, 273).

Those anticipated five years turned into thirty years and were to be for Coffin perhaps some of the most fruitful and most active years in his lifelong work against slavery. His Underground Railroad work was much more consuming in Cincinnati because of the city's proximity to Kentucky and the Ohio River. The Free Store effort, while not totally successful, at least helped to put a temporary crimp in the South's forced plantation labor. And, lastly, his work with the Freedmen's Aid Society, as the War Between the States accelerated, put a crown on his previous pre-Civil War work for the blacks.

Early Abolitionists in Cincinnati

4

Cincinnati had a history of violence associated with anti-slavery activity. Long before the Coffins arrived in 1847, many abolitionists in various walks of life had risked their livelihoods, even their lives, to aid escaping slaves.

In 1815, Benjamin Lundy, a twenty-six-year old Quaker, had organized the Union Humane Society, the first society with antislavery principles in Ohio. Another Quaker, Charles Osborn, began the publication of the *Philanthropist*, an antislavery paper, at Mt. Pleasant, Ohio, a short distance from Cincinnati and the first local settlement of Quakers from North Carolina in Ohio.

Other opponents of slavery, who lived in the Ohio River Valley, were the Presbyterian minister Rev. John Rankin and the freed slave John P. Parker. Rev. Rankin had left the south in 1821, freed his slaves, and settled in the little town of Ripley, Ohio, on the banks of the Ohio River. Runaways frequented Ripley, and in 1828 Rankin built a house on the crest of a hill in back of town, overlooking the Ohio River. For many years, lights burned in the windows of this parsonage and offered the fleeing slaves from Kentucky a welcome place to hide until transportation could be found to help them travel on. Later, Coffin took many of the slaves who first stopped at the Rankin House and passed them on north from Cincinnati. Some of the slaves also traveled the Underground Railroad north from Ripley through Mt.

Pleasant and Oberlin, another route on the way to safety. The John
Rankin Home still stands as an historic site and is open to the public.

John P. Parker was born into slavery in Norfolk, Virginia, in 1827.
He secured his freedom in 1845, moved to New Albany, Indiana and
then to Cincinnati, Ohio shortly thereafter. He, too, eventually came
to live in Ripley, Ohio and spent nearly fifteen years rescuing slaves.
The *Cincinnati Commercial Tribune*, as quoted in *His Promised
Land*, said of him, "...a more fearless creature never lived. He gloried
in danger...He would go boldly over into the enemy camp and filch
the fugitives to freedom" (Sprague 1997, 9).

Antislavery sympathizer James Gillespie Birney became a very
important mover in southwestern Ohio politics prior to Levi Coffin's
arrival. Birney had been involved in some violent agitation, fueling
the fire of the already rapidly accelerating Underground Railroad of
which Coffin would soon become a leader. A lawyer by education, a
journalist and publisher by trade, he was born in Danville, Kentucky
in 1792, of Presbyterian Scotch-Irish ancestry. His more radical
position on emancipation found him eventually an abolitionist in a
slave state. He came to Ohio in 1835, planning to establish an antislavery newspaper. Because of the commercial and social ties to
slaveholding communities, many Cincinnati citizens demanded that
Birney suppress his abolitionist views. The *Cincinnati Post, The Whig,*
and *The Republican* denounced Birney. Only Charles Hammond of
The Gazette supported the principle of the free press (Weisenberger
1941, 373).

Because of the antagonism prevalent among the citizens, Birney
decided to publish his paper, *The Philanthropist* (not to be confused
with Charles Osborn's *Philanthropist*), at the village of New Rich-

mond, up the river from Cincinnati. Southern Ohio was becoming the "battleground of opposing forces and Cincinnati naturally became the center of the struggle" (Craddock 1967, 98). After publishing his paper in New Richmond for about two years, threatened but never molested, Birney moved his publishing offices and press to Cincinnati.

Shortly after he set up his newspaper office at the corner of Main and Seventh Streets, a resolution was passed resolving that no abolition paper should be published or distributed in the town. Nevertheless, Birney printed *The Philanthropist* and on July 12, 1836, a rowdy crowd attacked the printing office and destroyed much of the premises. Birney continued to print. Once more, on July 30, a mob tore out the presses and materials and "defaced, 'pied' and partially destroyed" the property of the publisher, Mr. Achilles Pugh (Ford 1881, 87). Again, Birney, with friends, set up his presses for publication and printed *The Philanthropist*. This violence continued for months until, finally, a mob gathered on the corner of Main and Seventh Streets, marched to Birney's office, defaced an entrance, seized the press, and completely dismantled the establishment. They scattered part of the press and the types along Main Street and threw the rest into the river. The mob continued, intent on doing more mischief. They attacked homes of some blacks and destroyed their possessions.

Eventually, Birney moved on to Buffalo, New York, but he remained actively involved in politics and the antislavery cause and became, in 1840, Presidential candidate of the Free Soil Party, which avowed as its purpose the abolition of slavery.

By the 1830s, fifteen years before the Coffins' arrival, there was more talk about colonizing the slaves. Although Ohio was pledged to freedom by the Northwest Ordinance of 1787, in reality the state displayed a marked ambivalence toward slavery (Huff 1970, 4). There appeared to be a certain tacit tolerance of slavery, perhaps due directly to the state's linkage to the slave states, especially Kentucky, by close ties of kinship, culture and economics. Cincinnati was definitely a trading and manufacturing center of first importance. Much of the city's trade was with the South, so when the struggle over slavery became more intense, Cincinnati's financial interests were on the side of harmony and compromise.

An antislavery apologist, Theodore Weld, who later became instrumental in founding Lane Seminary in Cincinnati, wrote to James Birney on September 27, 1832 that he was convinced that colonization would "dissipate the horror of darkness which overhangs the southern country. [If it does not] we are undone" (Dumond 1938, 27). Weld was acting as a field agent for the New York merchant and reformer, Arthur Tappan, who had authorized Weld to find a site for a theological seminary in the West. Weld arrived in Cincinnati in the early 1830s to accept a beautiful, wooded tract of land in Walnut Hills, which had been donated by two merchants named Lane for the purpose of building just such a seminary. The State of Ohio contributed sums for its purpose and staffing. The teaching staff consisted of Arthur Tappan and noted scholars such as Lyman Beecher of Boston, who was persuaded to accept the presidency.

Beecher was an antislavery man, and many of Lane Seminary's students, who came from various sections of the country, spoke out with candor for the freeing of the slaves. Lane Seminary held public meetings voicing their belief that the duty of slaveholders was to emancipate their slaves immediately. At the conclusion of the series of meetings, a great swell of support appeared for immediate emancipation, a repudiation of colonization, and the formation of an abolition society.

In 1847, when Levi Coffin arrived in the city, Cincinnati defined all of the contradictions of the times regarding slavery. The city had become, disturbingly, no cradle of welcome for those seeking freedom. More than any other northern city, Cincinnati exhibited all the turmoil of the entire country within its borders. It was a microcosm of America. If Newport, Indiana had been an active terminal for the Coffins, Cincinnati would become more so.

The Cincinnati Free Store (1847-1857)

5

*"...free calicoes could seldom be called handsome,
even by the most enthusiastic; free umbrellas were hideous
to look at, and free candies, an abomination...,"*
—Lucretia Coffin Mott

Even as conscientious a Quaker woman as Lucretia Coffin Mott had a problem with the goods the Free Store could acquire and sell. From the beginning, Levi Coffin found it extremely difficult to discover sources of supplies in decent quantity and quality. While it was his greatest desire to spend more time managing his Free Store, he found the task almost insurmountable.

Levi and Catharine lived in a house in the city at Sixth and Elm Streets. Levi opened his Free Store adjacent to it on Elm Street, facing George Street. He soon moved to a larger building at Franklin and Broadway Streets. The executive committee of the Free Produce Association worked hard to locate supplies for the Free Store. They promised to raise at least three thousand dollars to help finance Coffin. They called three general meetings through the year to try to raise these additional funds (Nuermberger 1942, 51).

From the beginning, the Free Produce Store in Cincinnati was a struggle. Levi worked hard at making it a success. Once in Cincinnati, it did not take him long to investigate his sources for supplies, for to have his own Free Store succeed, it was necessary for him to have quick access to materials. He began to travel south to locate all the agents of the Free Produce Movements. He traveled to localities where slaves were not used to harvest cotton or sugar. After one such trip, he bought a three hundred dollar cotton gin in Cincinnati and shipped it to Mississippi, relying on it for free produced cotton. That gin became known as the "Abolition gin" and greatly stimulated the production of free-labor cotton (Ford 1984, 96-97).

The Philadelphia Association supplied the Free Store with all the cotton Levi Coffin could purchase. It was then made into fabric in Cincinnati. Coffin always felt that the first need was for "cheap prints, Calicoes that would cost in Philadelphia from eight to 12 or 14 cents per yard..." while brown muslin was next in demand (Nuermberger 1942, 98). Gould, Pearce & Co. spun the yarn, carpet warp, twine and candle wicking. They also put up looms and made brown muslin and other articles. The firm of Stearns and Foster made batting and wadding (Coffin 1898, 277). During 1848, Coffin purchased seven thousand dollars worth of cotton goods from the Philadelphia Free Produce Association. However, the Association was able to raise less than half the three thousand dollars, which they had promised to him.

Levi Coffin continued traveling through Tennessee and Mississippi, where he sought help in locating free labor material. He even eventually returned to North Carolina where he still had friends, some of whom welcomed his ideas and listened to his viewpoints on slavery. Along the way he was finding more and more advocates of the principles of the Free Produce Movement. But it was still extremely hard to make a living using this idea. Neuemberger, in her book, *The Free Produce Movement*, states that:

> ...The demand for free labor goods is somewhat difficult
> to assess. Demand would have been greater if the supply
> had been more adequate and satisfactory, while on the
> other hand, the supply could have been greatly increased
> if there had been sufficient demand to justify large-scale
> operations. Demand for the most was confined to Quak-
> ers, to a few earnest abolitionists of other denominations,
> and to those influenced by Quaker thought (Nuermberger
> 1942, 96-97).

If we could ask him today what he is most proud of in his life
work, Coffin would undoubtedly recite his years of Underground
Railroad successes. Yet, with all his concentration on spiriting the
fugitives away, he still tried to make a go of his Free Store, the reason
he had first come to Cincinnati in 1847. When the Coffins moved to a
larger home, they expanded the store, hoping to offer people the
option of buying only goods made and put together with free labor.
The challenge, of course, was that these goods had to be produced
with labor free of slave help: no cotton could be picked by slave
labor and no boats that used slaves as help could be used for shipping the goods.

It is probable that much of the profit of Coffin's Free Store went
into clothing and feeding the frightened mass of humanity who
showed up on his doorstep all hours of the day or night. "It seemed
to fall to our lot," he wrote, "to have such cares upon us, the most of
the time, for nearly twenty years after our removal to Cincinnati. It
was perhaps attributable, in part, to the fact that my wife and I had

been favored to overcome prejudice against color or caste" (Coffin 1898, 481).

Coffin's Free Produce Store was a losing business. He managed to keep up the business by close attention to financial affairs but had to sell it at the end of ten years and retire from the mercantile business in 1857. He retired with very limited means. He continued to work only by commission, receiving only limited consignments of country produce.

Coffin's Underground Railroad in Cincinnati (1847-1861) 6

When the Coffins had first arrived in Cincinnati, Levi was naively hopeful that his work with the Underground Railroad would not take up as much time as it had previously in Newport, Indiana. (Coffin 1898, 297). He soon realized it would be impossible to concentrate solely on his Free Store. Cincinnati, as noted earlier, was a hot bed of controversy. It would not have been possible for him to remain outside the work of the Underground Railroad. In fact, he was to devote the majority of his days and nights to this work.

On reading *Reminiscences*, it is extremely difficult to track Levi Coffin's early residences, although we know his original home and store was at Sixth and Elm Streets. We can surmise that he moved with his family several times within the first years of his transfer to Cincinnati. He had to find a spot ideal for hiding the slaves seeking his help or those given over to his care. Eventually, Levi Coffin operated more openly, but until he and Catharine became known (and until they came to know others they could trust) the Coffins remained very cautious about choosing their permanent site for their living quarters. Also, because of the few first-hand accounts of individual involvement in Underground Railroad activity, authenticity remains doubtful to researchers investigating known landmarks.

The house known to most researchers as the Levi Coffin house was at 3131 Wehrman Street, around the corner from the Lyman Beecher homestead. This house is no longer standing. It is likely that the Coffins lived there for a while between their arrival in 1847 and 1850, when the annual city directories began listing the locations of his homes. The home Levi mentions most often in *Reminiscences* was a large house on the southwest corner of Franklin and Broadway Streets, near what was then Woodward College.

The Woodward School for Performing Arts now stands on this site. A large plaque in the house identifies it as the location of one of Levi Coffin's homes. The plaque was placed there at the dedication of the building, when Levi Coffin's grandson was the speaker. This house had many rooms, and it was almost no problem to hide a slave, or more than one. Levi and Catharine eventually opened their home as a boarding house after a time in the city, and professors of religion of every denomination, teachers, and members from the Religious Society of Friends were the majority of its guests. Most were strongly antislavery. The Coffin home became almost a resort and very similar to the Friends Institute in London. With the number of guests always present, coming and going, activity and excitement day and night, it became a perfect depot for the Underground Railroad.

At times Catharine rapidly changed the dress of a woman fugitive and disguised her as a cook in their home. Some mulattos even passed as whites till they were safely out of the city. The most famous disguise on either man or woman was that of the Quaker, with the plain, light grey dress or suit, bonnet, with a veil, or brimmed hat, and a quiet downward tilt of the head. This disguise was a cunning deception that became more perfected the longer the Coffins and other abolitionists worked with the escaping slaves.

Because clothes and accessories were very important in deceiving slave hunters or pro-slavery supporters, women's groups disguised as "library associations," "reading circles," or "sewing circles" spent much of their time sewing and gathering clothes to disguise runaway slaves (Cosner 1991, 96). The two Sarah Ernsts, Mrs. Henry Miller, Mrs. Dr. [sic] Aydelott, Mrs. Julia Harwood, Mrs. Amanda Foster, Mrs. Elizabeth Coleman, Mrs. Mary Mann, Mrs. Mary Guild and Miss K. Emery were all mentioned by name in Coffin's *Reminiscences* as members of the Antislavery Sewing Society. These women met at the Coffin house every week for years to make suitable clothes for the fugitives.

Coffin pays tribute to all the women involved in aiding the abolitionists; those who hid the fugitives, cooked for them, sewed disguises for them, and/or shared their clothes with them. Women, who worked side by side with the men, were a very important element in the Underground Railroad's success story. Some women even traveled with the escapees till they were safely hidden. Laura Haviland, an abolitionist Quaker from Adrian, Michigan, and a frequent visitor and friend of Levi and Catharine Coffin's, would often accompany groups of fugitives out of Cincinnati, through the portal of escape in Toledo, and into safety in Michigan or Canada.

Harriet Beecher Stowe lived in Cincinnati for eighteen years and arrived at much of her antislavery sentiment from touching the lives of the blacks and associating with abolitionists within her circle of friends. Many researchers and scholars believe that the Quaker couple in *Uncle Tom's Cabin* represent Levi and Catharine Coffin. Coffin says himself that "from the fact that Eliza Harris was sheltered at our house several days, it was generally believed...that I and my wife were the veritable Simeon and Rachel Halliday" (Coffin 1898, 147-151). However, Wilbur H. Siebert in *The Underground Railroad* quotes Harriet Beecher Stowe, from her book *A Key to Uncle Tom's Cabin*, "...The character of Rachel Halliday was a real one, but she passed away to her reward. Simeon Halliday, calmly risking fine and imprisonment for his love to God and man, has had in this country many counterparts among the sect..." (Siebert 1898, 322).

The woman who worked closest to Levi, of course, was his wife Catharine. The Coffins were married more than fifty years and she worked by his side every step of the way. "Aunt Katy," as she was known to the slaves, was up at all hours with him, fixing food for the fugitives or making false beds or hiding young girls between bed slats. Coffin was not impervious to the debt he owed her in his work. He writes:

> Our attachment to each other was of long standing. She was an amiable and attractive young woman of lively, buoyant spirits. Her heart has ever been quick to respond to the cry of distress, and she has been an able and efficient helper to me in all my efforts on behalf of the fugitive slaves, and a cheerful sharer in all the toils, privations and dangers which we have, in consequence, been called upon to endure.
> (Coffin 1898, 103-104).

He also tells the story of the day there was a knock on the door, to which his wife answered. She spoke to the men who stood there: "What have you there?" One of them replied, "All Kentucky." "Well, bring all Kentucky in," she answered, then she stepped back to the room where Levi sat and said, "Get up, for all Kentucky has come" (Coffin 1898, 182-183).

The largest number of slaves ever seated at the Coffin table at one time was seventeen. It did not seem to rattle Catharine, as Levi again shares a moment when his wife was called on to stop her normal daily activity and help those who were knocking on her door.

...It was an interesting company, consisting of men and women, all apparently able-bodied and in the prime of life...They were all from the same neighborhood, a locality in Kentucky, some fifteen or twenty miles from the Ohio River, but belonged to different masters...they hurried on from station to station, traveling at night and hiding during the day, until they reached my house...On that morning my wife had risen first, and when she heard the two wagons drive up and stop, she opened the door...I said to one of the conductors: "The train has brought some valuable looking passengers this time. How many have you?"

"Only seventeen this load," he replied...My wife and our hired girl soon had breakfast prepared for the party, and the seventeen fugitives were all seated together around a long table in the dining room. We assured them that they could partake of their food without fear of molestation, for they were now among friends, in a neighborhood of abolitionists, and a fugitive had never been captured in our town...This interesting company of fugitives remained two days at my house to rest and prepare for their journey

northward. Having lost their bundles of clothing...many of
them were in need of garments and shoes. These were
furnished to them, and when all were made comfortable, I
arranged for teams and suitable conductors to take them
on to the next station (Coffin 1898, 178-184).

If the Coffins or any Quaker were asked, "Do you have a slave in
your house?" they could honestly answer "No," for there was no such
thing as a slave to a Quaker. There is a story told about a couple,
John and Mary Smith, who were hiding two women fugitives, when
some slavehunters arrived. While John answered the door, Mary took
the girls into the bedroom, pulled the bed apart, lifted the mattress,
and whispered for the girls to lie down on the ropes that supported
the mattress. Mrs. Smith remade the bed over the girls and went
downstairs. "Let them come in, John," she told her husband. "Thee
knows there are no slaves here." According to her beliefs, Mrs. Smith
had not lied. (Cosner 1991, 101).

For Levi and Catharine Coffin, once committed to the cause of the
slave, their work never ceased.

...[We] did not lack for work. Our willingness to aid the
slaves was soon known, and hardly a fugitive came to the
city without applying to us for assistance. There seemed to
be a continual increase of runaways...and I was obliged to
devote a large share of time from my business to making
arrangements for the concealment and safe conveyance of
the fugitives. They sometimes came to the door frightened
and panting and in a destitute condition, having fled in
such haste and fear that they had no time to bring any

clothing except what they had on, and that was often very scant. The expense of providing suitable clothing for them when it was necessary for them to go on immediately, or of feeding them when they were obliged to be concealed for days or weeks, was very heavy. Added to this was the cost of hiring teams when a party of fugitives had to be conveyed out of the city by night to some Underground Railroad depot, from twenty to thirty miles distant. The price for a two-horse team on such occasions was ten dollars, and sometimes two or three teams were required. ...Our house was large, and well adapted for secretive fugitives. Very often slaves would lie concealed in upper chambers for weeks, without the boarders or frequent visitors at our house knowing anything about it. My wife had a quiet, unconcerned way of going about her work, as if nothing unusual was on hand, which was calculated to lull every suspicion of those who might be watching, and who would have been at once aroused by any sign of secrecy or mystery. Even the intimate friends of the family did not know when there were slaves secreted in the house, unless they were directly informed.

When my wife took food to the fugitives she generally concealed it in a basket, and put some freshly ironed garment on the top, to make it look like a basketful of clean clothes. Fugitives were not often allowed to eat in the kitchen, from fear of detection (Coffin 1898, 578-579).

Of all the abolitionists in Cincinnati, Quaker or otherwise, Coffin and his wife Catharine were the nucleus around which all antislavery activity revolved. A horse and wagon was always on hand. They never slept without anticipating a knock on the door. Did they seek the excitement? Perhaps, a little. Did they tire of it? Undoubtedly. Did they quit? Never. It is evident that their work continued up to, into and beyond the Civil War. As long as they were needed, they were there for the disenfranchised, who sought freedom above life.

There is significant evidence that the slavehunters following the fleeing refugees bestowed the title "President of the Underground Railroad" on Levi Coffin. Just when they began calling him by that title is not known. It can be surmised that its origin developed from the inability of the slavehunters, or bloodhounds, to ever get the slightest intelligence of their slaves after they reached the Coffin house.

Coffin happily accepted this title and further said he would "accept any other position they were disposed to give me on that road—conductor, engineer, fireman, or brakeman" (Coffin 1898, 189-190). As far as he was aware there was "not one instance when a fugitive [entrusted to his care] was captured and taken back into slavery" (Coffin 1898, 120). Wilbur H. Siebert, says that "...the genial but fearless Quaker came to be known generally by the fictitious but happy title, President of the Underground Railroad" (Siebert 1898, 111).

Though often discouraged and most likely tired, Coffin never lost the original fire that had energized him as a boy in North Carolina. His inherent belief in equality increased the more he came in contact with the black slaves' intellectual capabilities, their love for their families, their spiritual relationship with God, their need for love and acceptance. Though his work expanded and changed as the Civil War approached, he proudly wore his legendary title of President of the Underground Railroad all his life. He is said to have "resigned" his title after the Civil War started, but he never resigned his promise to be there for the individuals of this captive race. His acceptance of the role he played in the ultimate freedom for the slave became part of his bones, as much a part of himself as his Quaker hat. "I was burdened with them because others could not be found to take them, and because, out of compassion, I could not refuse" (Coffin 1898, 578-579).

The Quaker manner of answering conflict is unique: the art of "gentle persuasion." His was a rare face that could smile at the slavehunters as well as the hunted, speak softly without a weapon, turn the "bloodhounds" away, and still maintain a sense of humor, which only befuddled his enemies and confused the haughty. Many of the remembered escapes he included in his book are laced with the subtlety of humor, as well as pathos. The picture of Levi Coffin, as a staid, somber Quaker has to be misleading, for he was able to laugh and offer a light piece of advice or trickery in so many disastrous cases where impatience, anger, or ill-humor would have killed the outcome. The seriousness of his work, the lives put in his hands, must have been an awesome responsibility to a man of his ideals. Coffin drew upon the singular gift of his sense of fun, that playful quality which lightened his burden and kept him sane, to conquer the evil he confronted. At one point he quotes his wife as having "reproved me for being mischievous" (Coffin 1898, 604).

Two of the more whimsical accounts that he shares in his *Remi-*

niscences relate specifically to hats. Hats were an important part of the dress of a member of the Religious Society of Friends. It is only fitting that the stories of the hats evidence Coffin's love of teasing and the enjoyment he derived from tricking his enemies.

On one occasion, he was present at a fugitive slave trial. His hat remained on his head as he stood at the side of the room viewing the proceedings. Several times a marshal commanded him to remove his hat. Each time Coffin paid no attention to him. "I command you to take off your hat, sir!" the marshal said more loudly. In a low voice Coffin answered him, "What is the matter with my hat? I suppose that it will not hurt anybody." Again the marshal said, "I have authority. I command you to pull off your hat." This time Coffin replied, "I will not pull off my hat to accommodate thee. It is not my habit nor the habit of my people to make obeisance to men."

The banter continued until the marshal angrily jerked the hat off Coffin's head. The marshal offered it to him but Coffin did not take it, saying, "I thought thou wanted my hat." He left the marshal standing there, looking foolish, until the hat was finally laid on a side table. Finally a policeman who knew Coffin suggested that Coffin better go and retrieve his hat. "I did not put it there, and I shall not go after it," he said. Finally the policeman brought the hat to Coffin, who placed it again on his head. The marshal was furious and again commanded Coffin to remove his hat. The same type of conversation ensued until the marshal again pulled the hat off of Coffin's head. This time a city officer insisted the marshal return the hat. Coffin accepted it again, placed it on his head and kept it there. The Cincinnati papers carried a report of this incident the following day and Coffin writes of the laughs he and his friends had sharing the good humor of the day before. Many asserted he had whipped the marshal. "I didn't hurt a hair of his head," Coffin lightly replied (Coffin 1898, 569-574).

A second experience with hats occurred again at a fugitive slave trial. A slave man named Lewis escaped from Kentucky and came to Cincinnati and then to Columbus, but was tracked down by his master, who brought him back to Cincinnati to ultimately return him to slavery. Coffin and John Jolliffe, a lawyer and friend of the slaves, immediately secured a writ to arrest the master for kidnapping. The case went to trial.

The courtroom was crowded with interested persons, both white and black. The room was long and had a table through the center. On one side of the table was a crowd of black people, standing; the judge and lawyers sat at the table, the slave opposite them, and behind the slave stood a crowd of white people, mostly friends of the slave.

Lewis, the slave, was crowded, so to gain more room, he slipped his chair back a little way. Since no one noticed, he slipped it back a little further, and a little further, until he was almost into the crowd. Coffin observed the movement, and together with other abolitionist friends, encouraged him to action. They placed a good Quaker hat on his head and he stepped into the crowd of black people and then through the door. It was not until five minutes after he left that his absence was discovered. The marshal made a dash down the steps but the fugitive had disappeared. A search was made for him but the hunters never found him.

Coffin and other abolitionists knew he would make his way to Avondale, where the sexton of the black burying ground would hide him. So quickly they found him, disguised him in woman's apparel and brought him to the house of black friends on Broadway, near Sixth Street, where he remained a week. Then Lewis was again disguised in a woman's dress. He walked down Broadway to the corner of Eighth Street. There he saw Coffin, who continued to walk on to Vine Street and joined a crowd of people walking to evening services. Lewis was following but not near enough to be seen with Coffin. Coffin entered the basement of the church and Lewis followed. He was hidden in one of the church rooms literally for weeks, since he was still being hunted. Finally, a Presbyterian minister and his wife offered to take Lewis out of the city in their horse and carriage. Lewis, still disguised as a woman, a veil covering his face, was met at the church and taken about thirty miles out of the city to a depot of the Underground Railroad. He ultimately went to Sandusky and then on to Canada, where he arrived safely (Coffin 1898, 548-552).

It is documented in Coffin's *Reminiscences*, as well as Laura Haviland's memoir, *A Woman's Life-Work*, that Coffin often traveled north to Michigan and Canada to visit some of the escaped fugitives whom he helped along the way. This follow-up was popular with those who had made it to freedom, for they loved to see him come and would spontaneously hug and make over him. Inevitably he always discovered more work to be done. These refugees needed housing. They needed food. They needed to earn money and to educate themselves. He found himself calling on additional persons to help in their settlement. He continued to feel as responsible for this aspect of their journey as he had for its beginning. He searched out people and associations that could help provide food, clothing, and housing for these freed men and women.

Quakers were not the only abolitionists. Coffin was willing to work with all peoples of whatever race and religious affiliation in the peaceful undercover activity of the Underground Railroad. Without others of differing religious persuasions many escapes would not have been successful. The denominations most prominent in Cincinnati as helpers in the cause were particularly Presbyterians, Baptists, and Methodists. Cincinnati also had a unique element of German descendents who emigrated and settled there. Many Quakers were, themselves, of German descent. Wilbur H. Siebert quotes Lyman Goodnow, an Underground Railroad worker, as saying, that "in cases of emergency the Germans were the next best to Quakers for protection" (Siebert 1898, 92). Few if any Germans ever owned slaves. Yet, in *Quakers and Southern Slavery*, Stephen B. Weeks says "if God in His wisdom raises up nations to a certain end, then this is true of institutions as well. The mission of Quakerism has been to the slave…They announced their opposition to the system when it had no other opponents, and they steadfastly maintained their testimony until its last traces were swept from the English-speaking world" (Weeks 1968, 198).

It is hard to believe that there were not some workers on the Underground Railroad lines who suffered physical harm or even lost their lives to the cause of helping slaves escape. Coffin speaks often of a John Fairfield, whose radical, aggressive approach to freeing the slaves was in direct opposition to Coffin's. Coffin often chastised him for carrying guns and for accepting money from some escaping blacks so they could be reunited with their families. Fairfield went heavily armed, and he used his weapons when necessary. He also was killed on one of his escape ventures.

Coffin never speaks of being physically hurt in any way. He did receive many threats during his work with the Underground Railroad. He once received anonymous letters warning him that his store, porkhouse, and dwelling would be burned to the ground. One letter from Kentucky said that a body of armed men were on their way to destroy the town and warned him to flee or be killed. He and his friends stood firm, refusing to be intimidated. On the night the men were to come, he and his family retired to bed as usual. They did not have watches appointed around the house to guard their lives. He said they slept peacefully. In the morning the buildings were still all there and the threatened destruction had not taken place. Sometimes, of course, the threats did lead to violence in other parts of town. One time the slave owners forced their way into some houses where they believed there were slaves being hidden and threw brickbats and stones through windows. Antagonism, hatred, and fear lead many times to disaster and, it can be supposed, even death. That the Coffins were saved from severe harm was a tribute to the protection they must have had from friends and associates who supported their work, as well as from the respect that even the slavehunters had for Coffin.

A History of the State of Ohio gives credit to the Ohio Quakers' unfailing and undying selflessness by referring to "two or three areas...having a modest Quaker element [which] exercised an influence disproportionate to its numbers" (Roseboom 1944, 219). Without a doubt, Coffin's work in the southwestern part of the state was a primary influence. A week before President Lincoln's assassination, in 1865, Lincoln was reported to have said that he had been "only an instrument in the freeing of the slaves. The credit for emancipation belonged to the ...logic and moral power of Garrison and the antislavery of the people of the country" (Sterling 1991, 1).

In 1861, Cincinnati residents could feel the weight of the coming rebellion. Coffin's work had remained brisk up to the time of the Civil War. He continued to assist free blacks to purchase relatives still being held slaves. He also increased his help for the poor and the sick among the fugitive families of the city. "I was no respecter of color or race," he wrote in *Reminiscences*.

> I was often accused by those who were prejudiced against colored people, of thinking more of the colored race than I did of the white...Sometimes I heard people say that they would not have a Negro about them; they had never hired one that did them any good...I replied that my experience had been different...I often gave them employment in preference to whites, not that I felt any greater attachment to them on account of their color, but because I knew that they were often unjustly refused and neglected...
> (Coffin 1898, 577-578).

His work with the Underground Railroad took on even greater intensity and purpose, for the fugitives were now fleeing in increasing numbers. The difference was that now much of the Underground Railroad activity was done "above" ground. The feeling of antipathy toward the abolitionists began to fade, and citizens of Ohio seemed much more disposed to aiding a fugitive.

Prior to the actual beginning of the Civil War, Cincinnati had preferred, if only for economic reasons, a peaceful resolution of the slavery question. Now that war was at their doorstep, they had to abandon that hope and respond to Lincoln's call for volunteers. Soon there was an army of more than one hundred thousand men in Cincinnati ready to protect the city against the rebel army. Many of these men were untrained soldiers, without any preparation for camping or supplies for provisions. Although the Coffins did not believe in war and fighting, they did believe in the cause and always believed in helping to care for the sick and hungry. "During the excitement our house was more like a military post than a depot of the Underground Railroad... We had a number of boarders," Coffin reports, "all the men armed themselves and reported for service...they placed their guns by their bedsides, when the alarm was sounded on the fire-bells in the night, they sprang up, seized their weapons and hurried to their post" (Coffin 1898, 600-606). Canons were placed on Mount Adams and other high hills above and below the city, to bombard the river if the Southern army attempted to cross.

On April 12, 1861, Fort Sumter was fired upon. Levi and Catharine Coffin prepared at once "to feed the hungry and to clothe the naked." Coffin and his friends set up tables in the market houses, in the parks, and on the public sidewalks so those who were defending the city could eat. They spread a table on the sidewalk of Franklin Street from Broadway to Sycamore—in front of the Coffin house and Woodward College—where they could feed five hundred people at one time. The Coffin basement kitchen became the depository for the extra food between meals. They warmed coffee and tea on their large cooking stove. Regiments of volunteers from Indiana and other northwestern states passed through Cincinnati on their way south and east. Soon the Coffin house was being used as a hospital, since beds were scarce. Coffin remembers, "It was not long until our services were needed in caring for sick and wounded soldiers brought here from various Southern battlefields, …We nursed them carefully until they were able to go to their homes …we took in sick soldiers and cared for them until they were able to travel, feeling that it was our duty to do so" (Coffin 1898, 605). Nearly every night the Coffins had soldiers to attend to. Steamboats from Cincinnati, with doctors and surgeons on board, traveled south to care for and, if necessary, remove the wounded. Many were brought back to Cincinnati, where the Coffins quickly and generously gave them succor. Their home now was a different type of terminal but one still that welcomed all persons, no matter what color, creed, or religious denomination.

The Final Call (1862-1877)

7

By the fall of 1862, the Civil War had fully opened west of the mountains. While the war progressed, it seemed the northerners forgot about escaping slaves. Many times slaves were just abandoned or taken further south to fend for themselves. At times boats left slaves at the Cincinnati wharf without food or shelter. Levi Coffin was called upon frequently for help. He saw a new need and immediately began to investigate the best way to help these destitute blacks, who were now being left alone in many cases to die or seek shelter together in abandoned warehouses or cellars. Most of them had to beg or steal scraps of food to keep from starving. He wrote to his friends in Indiana and Ohio and began to collect bedding, clothing and money. The Cincinnati Merchant's Exchange, a business association, called a meeting to plan an organization to aid these "freedmen," who were now trying to live together in camps. They formed the Contraband Relief Organization, whose membership came from many different religious denominations. The members of this organization were mostly philanthropic businessmen with antislavery connections, including a large number of both men and women from the Religious Society of Friends. Coffin was appointed administrator, even though many feared he would be too radical. At this point in his life, Coffin began the last phase of his work for the African American refugees, one that would last almost until his death.

At first the normal confusion in setting up an organization reigned. Some citizens were worried that financial support for an increased number of freedmen would all "come out of the pockets of the tax-payers" (Halliday 1964, 172). An alleged official order given by General Grant to send all refugees to Ohio proved to be a rumor, but other gossip and internal discord had to be settled before work could begin. Some members of the organization, Coffin included, believed education should be given to these freed blacks, as well as food and blankets. Yet, education, others argued, would alienate too many Northerners. A split in the Contraband Relief Association ensued. The Western Freedmen's Aid Commission was formed with Coffin as general agent in January, 1863, the same month as Lincoln's Emancipation Proclamation. The Western Freedmen's Aid Commission became chiefly devoted to education, while the first association continued to be primarily concerned with relief. The Contraband Relief Association collected supplies such as clothing, shoes, blankets, yard goods, seeds and Bibles. Concerned citizens donated money so the organization could purchase thread, scissors, medicines, and soap. Somehow the participants gradually found textbooks, slates, and teachers to further the cause of the freed slave. By 1864 the two organizations combined much of their effort and worked more with each other for the betterment of the destitute blacks. The chief sources of relief came from the various Friends meetings, not only in Ohio and Indiana, but also in New York, Missouri, and eventually, London, England. The Shakers at Union Village, Warren County, Ohio supplied the large packets of seeds sought by the Commission (Halliday 1964, 175).

Coffin gave General Grant credit for securing free transportation for all supplies for the freedmen and for the agents and teachers as well. This organization eventually opened schools among the freed slaves, as well as supplying necessities for the newly displaced African Americans. Despite Coffin's lack of enthusiasm for further travel, he believed he had to try to encourage a more active participation in this mission. Reluctantly he accepted the job of visiting others throughout the country and even England to beg for supplies to aid the cause. He traveled to Nashville and points in Tennessee (then occupied by the Union troops), where the freed blacks had gathered by the thousands. Demand was far exceeding the supply. He encouraged Friends in Indiana and Ohio to increase their donations. Supplies did increase for a while but still the need grew.

Many masters shot their slaves as the Union troops approached. Freed slaves and more wounded runaways arrived at camps. Levi Coffin traveled all over the South, helping to organize schools and shelter and hospital care for the freedmen. Whenever he returned to Cincinnati he had no time to rest. He spent his days shipping boxes of clothing, bedding, books, and other articles to the freedmen and wrote letters through the night. Because of the increasing number of freedmen coming to Cincinnati from the South, Coffin petitioned the government for a tract of land to build a home where they could live until places could be found for them. The government complied, and erected a building at their expense and ordered rations and medical help. The Western Freedmen's Aid Commission furnished clothing, bedding and books and also employed teachers to help. The Commission kept this building open for three years.

In May of 1864, Coffin embarked on a trip to England in an effort to solicit more help for this new cause. He departed with a letter of

recommendation from Henry Ward Beecher, who then lived in
Maine. He received his passport from Secretary Salmon P. Chase, the
former Cincinnati antislavery lawyer who had argued many fugitive
slave trials with Coffin. The freedmen had many friends with Cincinnati roots who were now in positions of influence in government and
whose original support and pledge to help would not be forgotten.
Coffin, himself, felt inadequate for public speaking, so he was not
really looking forward to the trip. Solicitation work was not his style,
begging for money and being in the public eye was not something he
aspired to. He would have been just as happy never to have to go to
London. His voice was weak and his aging health feeble. He was
afraid that he could not extend his voice over an audience in a large
church or public building. Members of the London Yearly Meeting of
Friends, however, welcomed him and gradually eased his personal
concerns. His London mission was not just to the Religious Society of
Friends. It was non-sectarian and included a vast number of other
denominational members. His son, Henry, accompanied him. Coffin
wrote in his *Reminiscences*:

> I felt lonely and depressed in spirit. I reflected that I was a
> stranger in the great city of London,...I had been a worker
> and not a speaker in the antislavery cause; I had always
> avoided public speaking or prominence of any kind, yet
> the work before me seemed to demand the very qualifica-
> tions which I felt I lacked. A sense of the great responsibil-
> ity resting upon me weighed me down. I felt that I was
> unequal to the task...I prayed earnestly for divine guid-
> ance and direction...
> (Coffin 1898, 658-659).

This heavenly guidance for which he prayed must have indeed comforted him. It is evident that he regained his former humor and love of teasing. He recalled one incident where he was asked about the disposition of the freed slaves. "Do they help themselves?" they asked him. "I replied that they did not wish to become paupers. However, there is quite a difference among them; some are nearly as trifling and worthless as white people" (Coffin 1898, 666-667). Despite his misgivings, his trip to the Continent was a success. He returned with over $100,000 in supplies and money, quite a sum in 1864. The Cincinnati Freedmen Association maintained its own identity until 1870, when the Missionary Association took it over. Coffin continued as an agent of that society for several more years.

On March 30, 1870, Congress adopted the Fifteenth Amendment, which gave the black man the right to vote. It was the last of the three amendments that finally abolished slavery and recognized the citizenship of the African American. Article XIII, proclaimed and adopted in 1865, was the first amendment in sixty-one years. It abolished slavery and involuntary servitude, except for crime, everywhere in the United States or any place subject to the jurisdiction of the United States. Article XIV, adopted in 1868, named all persons born or naturalized in the United States as citizens of the United States and of the state in which they reside. And finally, Article XV recognized these citizens' right to a voice in the ballot box. It stated that the right of citizens of the United States to vote shall not be denied by the United States on account of "race, color, or previous condition of servitude."[1]

[1] By these three amendments "the chains of the Constitution" as Jefferson called its limitations, were placed upon the states as they had previously been on the Federal Government (Norton 1941, 250). As much danger of inordinate power existed within the states as it did within the Federal Government. The issue of debate in Congress for three years was brought to a close, but only by the narrowest margin. It was ratified by a majority of one vote in the Senate and two in the house (Roseboom 1944, 471).

When the Fifteenth Amendment was adopted the black people of Cincinnati celebrated and Levi Coffin was one of the many who made speeches. It was at this time that he officially resigned his title as President of the Underground Railroad, the title that he had held for more than thirty years. "The title was given to me," he wrote,

> by slavehunters who could not find their fugitive slaves after they got into my hands. I accepted the office thus conferred upon me, and have endeavored to perform my duty faithfully. Government has now taken the work of providing for the slaves out of our hands. The stock of the Underground Railroad has gone down in the market, the business is spoiled, the road is of no further use.
> ...I resign my office and declare the operations of the Underground Railroad at an end (Coffin 1898, 712).

An account written in the *Evening Star* while Coffin was visiting England says of him, "for thirty-three years he received into his house more than one hundred slaves every year. These slaves he housed, clothed, and when sick attended them, and when they died buried them" (Coffin 1898, 694). Larry Gara, in *Liberty Line*, says that, when writing his memoirs, Coffin "used letters and other documents to supplement his memory, but the aged reformer admitted that errors would appear and asked his readers to pardon them because of his 'advanced age and feebleness'. Nevertheless, and despite his evident exaltation of his own role as reputed president, Coffin's description of the Underground Railroad in Indiana and western Ohio is one of the more reliable firsthand accounts..." (Gara 1961, 175).

Levi Coffin died at his home in Avondale, at 2:30 p.m. September 16, 1877. He was 79 years old. The *Cincinnati Daily Gazette* wrote: "The great question with him was not, is it popular? but is it right? At no period of his life was there ever a spirit of gloominess; but ever pleasant and happy; enjoying life's blessings, and looking joyfully to the grand results in the future" (Coffin 1898, 729).

It is incredible Levi Coffin lived to such an age, considering the risks he took all his life. Four children had died ahead of him; two lived, Henry and Jesse. Catharine, his wife, with whom he celebrated his golden wedding anniversary, also survived him. The following excerpt appeared in the *Cincinnati Daily Gazette*, following Coffin's funeral:

> The funeral of Levi Coffin, the philanthropist, drew an
> over-flowing audience to the Friends Meeting House,
> corner of Eighth and Mound streets, at eleven o'clock
> yesterday morning. Among the congregation were several
> of his surviving associates in antislavery work, his associ-
> ates in the Freedmen's Aid Commission, and dusky, tear-
> bedewed faces of members of the once oppressed race,
> for whose emancipation he strove so long and earnestly...
> The casket of plain black walnut, with four black bar
> handles, was borne into the meeting-house by eight pall-
> bearers, of whom Ezra Bailey and Mr. Geo. D. Smith are
> members of the Society of Friends, the Rev. R.S. Rust and
> the Rev. J.M.Walden were old co-workers with the
> deceased, and Mr. George Peterson, Robert Scott, Peter H.
> Clark and T. Colston are colored men....

The Rev. Dr. Rust, Secretary of the Freedmen's Aid Society of the M.E.Church, spoke of the deceased friend's thorough unselfishness. He had too great a mission to perform to spare any time to take care of himself, and God took care of him. He was an honest, wise, and judicious man-

…

…At the close of Dr. Walden's remarks…the body was then conveyed to the Quaker burying-ground on West Fork, near Cumminsville, followed by a large concourse of friends (Coffin 1898, 727-730).

Many whose lives touched the dispossessed during the pre-Civil War years in Ohio and Indiana moved on to spend their remaining days elsewhere. But Levi Coffin stayed where he had done so much of his work. It is common that a Quaker grave was unmarked or at least had no standing headstone to honor its inhabitant. But the publication, *150 Years of Cincinnati Monthly Meetings of the Society of Friends, July 11, 1902*, records that "on Decoration Day 5th Month 30, 1902, a suitable monument 6 feet high and 2 feet square, was unveiled by the colored people of Cincinnati." The inscription reads:

Levi Coffin died 9th Month 16, 1877 in his 78th year, a
Christian Philanthropist. Catherine Coffin died 5th Month
22, 1881, in her 78th year. Her work well done! Noble
Benefactors!! Aiding thousands to gain freedom, a tribute
from the colored people of Cincinnati, Ohio (Kephart, 29).

John Greenleaf Whittler was the foremost Quaker poet of Nineteenth Century America, noted for his antislavery sentiment and for
his fearless voice in support of emancipation. The eleven stanzas
below, from "In Remembrance of Joseph Sturge," were selected from
the complete twenty-five stanza poem, to be read at the burial of Levi
Coffin in the Quaker burying ground near Cumminsville, Ohio*. It
clearly was chosen to honor both Levi Coffin and John Greenleaf
Whittier. I include it here for identical reasons.

In Remembrance of Joseph Sturge

...Thanks for the good man's beautiful example,
Who in the vilest saw
Some sacred crypt or altar of a temple
Still vocal with God's law;

And heard with tender ear the spirit sighing
As from its prison cell,
Praying for pity, like the mournful crying
Of Jonah out of hell.

Not his the golden pen's or lip's persuasion,
But a fine sense of right,
And truth's directness, meeting each occasion
Straight as a line of light.

His faith and works, like streams that intermingle,
In the same channel ran;
The crystal clearness of an eye kept single
Shamed all the frauds of man.

The very gentlest of all human natures
He joined to courage strong,
And love outreaching unto all God's creatures
With sturdy hate of wrong.

Tender as woman; manliness and meekness
In him were so allied
That they who judged him by his strength or weakness
Saw but a single side.

Men failed, betrayed him, but his zeal seemed nourished
By failure and by fall;
Still a large faith in human-kind he cherished,
And in God's love for all.

And now he rests: his greatness and his sweetness
No more shall seem at strife;
And death has moulded into calm completeness
The statue of his life.

Where the dews glisten and the song-birds warble,
　　His dust to dust is laid,
In nature's keeping, with no pomp of marble,
　　To shame his modest shade.

The forges glow, the hammers all are ringing;
　　Beneath its smoky vale,
Hard by, the city of his love is swinging
　　Its clamorous iron flail.

And round his grave are quietude and beauty,
　　And the sweet heaven above, -
The fitting symbols of a life of duty
　　Transfigured into love!

* Many years later Levi and Catharine Coffin were reinterred in Spring Grove Cemetery in Cincinnati.

Epilogue

"A prophet is not without honor, save in his own country" (Matthew 13: Vs.57). This could certainly *not* be said of Levi Coffin, either in life or death. He was duly honored, appreciated, and loved by his friends and by all those he helped, either for a minute or for days, on their way to freedom. These people knew Coffin's worth and were generous in their praise.

The *Christian Press* printed the following:

'FRIEND LEVI COFFIN GONE HOME'

Levi Coffin, well known to many of our readers personally and to nearly all of them by reputation, has been called by the Master "to go up higher." He died at his residence in Avondale, September 16, in the seventy-ninth year of his age. The words of King David may be fitly applied to him: "Know ye not that there is a prince and a great man fallen this day in Israel?" Few men have accomplished more in the cause of humanity than he has done. ...The poor and oppressed always found in him a sympathetic friend...If he had devoted the talents, including the large measure of common sense with which he was endowed, to the pursuit of wealth, he would doubtless have left behind

him tens of thousands of dollars...He counted it a wiser
thing to alleviate the distress of these fellow-men around
him,...Now, heaven has one more attraction for the
thousands of friends he has left behind (Coffin 1898, 731-
732).

Do the citizens of Cincinnati today know enough about Coffin or
the other abolitionists who worked so hard for the freedom of the
blacks? It is easy, but disastrous, to ignore the past. It leaves a void
in the understanding of the present and prevents effective preparation
for the future. Yet, who speaks of Coffin today, or even studies the
important contribution he and other abolitionists made to Cincinnati
and the surrounding area in Ohio and Indiana between 1800 and
1870?

Credit must be given to Fountain City, Indiana, formerly Newport,
Indiana, Levi Coffin's first home on moving west from North Carolina.
In 1967 the State of Indiana purchased the home Levi and Catharine
Coffin built in 1839. Through the efforts of the Levi Coffin House
Association today, the historic site is open to the public and is
maintained and preserved to honor Levi and Catharine Coffin's
antislavery work. It is the only building left standing which is known
to have been involved in their lives either in North Carolina, Fountain
City, Indiana, or Cincinnati, Ohio. (The Levi Coffin House, National
Historic Landmark, Fountain City, Indiana, 1839-1847, pamphlet.)

What happened to the buildings and where are the landmarks of
those disturbing early days between 1800 and 1870 in Cincinnati?
Sadly, most are rubble, or lost to absolute identification. Much of the
Ohio River's bank is now covered with stadiums, power stations,

parks and parking lots. Escape routes have been covered over with pavement, housing projects, and suburban malls. The past, however, cannot really be buried. It is always there, beckoning us to remember; to encounter, and to honor good men and women who fought for justice.

Today, monuments, walls of names, and statues are erected so we will not forget these good people. In the war against injustice and slavery there are many to credit for victory, not the least of which are the blacks themselves, who wanted freedom and took the risk to find it. At last, the nation seems to be recognizing this pre-Civil War era as important as any in the history of the nation. More is being written about this era, more cities are paying tribute to citizens who brought slavery to an end. Now Cincinnati, Ohio has dedicated itself to restoring and remembering that distinctive period of history so much a part of its city's heritage. It is committed to seeing that this epoch of history will not be forgotten. Men and women of all races in government, business, education and differing religious denominations are coming together to build an Underground Railroad Freedom Center on Cincinnati's riverfront. The Freedom Center, scheduled to open in the spring of 2004, will celebrate the courage and cooperation of all who ran the Underground Railroad as a secret network to help slaves escape to freedom. It will focus on that particular quality of self-determination among blacks necessary for the flight to freedom and its purpose will also be to educate and inspire racial understanding among citizens of all cultures. The Ohio River in Cincinnati, which was both the legal and symbolic dividing line between slave South and free North is the perfect site.

There is a proverb: "History repeats itself." And the hands of time move slowly. When we read about the treatment of a minority, do we question whether man ever learns from his mistakes? To quote again the greatest Quaker poet of his age, John Greenleaf Whittier, in his poem, *Raphael*:

> The tissue of the Life to be
> We weave with colors all our own,
> And in the field of Destiny
> We reap as we have sown.

Will the nation always be reaping and repairing? Will America always be working to eradicate a wrong, correct an injustice, close the book on a history that proves so difficult to erase from time, even one hundred or more years after Coffin's intense labor to extend freedom and justice? Witness Martin Luther King's plea in the 1960s. What time was it, 1960 or 1860? Does America yet understand? Consider these questions which we may yet have to answer. It makes a life like Levi Coffin's much more singular in its total commitment to lifting a suffering people out of the dark hole of suffering and inhumanity.

Appendix A

FUGITIVE SLAVE ACTS

First Fugitive Slave Act
"An Act Respecting Fugitives from Justice
and Persons Escaping from the Service of their Masters"
1793

(abbreviated form)

Section 1 – No person held to service or labor in one state, under the laws thereof, escaping into another, shall, in consequence of any law or regulation therein, be discharged from such service or labor, but shall be delivered up on claim of the party to whom such service or labor may be due.

Section 2 – If any person or persons shall rescue the fugitive, the person or persons so offending shall, on conviction, be fined not exceeding five hundred dollars, and be imprisoned not exceeding one year.

Section 3 – When a person held to labor in any of the United States shall escape into any other state, the person who is owed the labor, or his agent or attorney, is empowered to seize or arrest such fugitive, and take him or her before any judge and upon proof, return said fugitive to the state or territory from which he or she fled.

Section 4 – Any person who knowingly obstructs such an arrest or shall rescue such a fugitive from labor, shall pay the sum of $500.00.

Second Fugitive Slave Act
"An act to amend the act approved February 12, 1793"
September 18, 1850

Section 1 – Persons who are authorized to exercise the role of justice of the peace, or other magistrates of any kind in the United States, may arrest, imprison or bail under the same act of the twenty-four of September 1789.

Section 2 – The Superior Court of each territory shall have the same power to appoint commissioners to take depositions of witnesses in civil causes ,and they shall all have the same powers, and exercise the same duties conferred by law upon the commissioners.

Section 3 – The Circuit Courts shall enlarge the number of commissioners with a view to afford reasonable facilities to reclaim fugitives from labor, and to afford the prompt discharge of the duties imposed by this act.

Section 4- The commissioners above named shall have authority to take and remove such fugitives from service or labor to the state or territory from which such persons may have escaped or fled.

Section 5 – It shall be the duty of all marshals to obey and execute all warrants, or be fined in the sum of one thousand dollars. In conformity with this act, all good citizens are hereby commanded to aid and assist in the prompt and efficient execution of this law.

Section 6 – When a person held to service or labor in any state has escaped into another state, the persons to whom the service is due may pursue and reclaim such fugitive person, either by warrant, or by seizing and arresting such fugitive, where the same can be done without process.

The remaining four sections continue to legally boost the absolute authority of the slaveholder over any fleeing slave. It was estimated that at least six thousand fugitives fled their homes to Canada immediately after this Second Fugitive Slave Act. (Siebert, *The Underground Railroad*.)

Appendix B

THE BLACK LAWS[*]
January 5, 1804

1. No Negro was permitted after the following June to settle or reside in the state unless he first produced a certificate from some court attesting his freedom.

2. Every Negro residing within the state was required, on or before the first day of the following June, to record his name in the county clerk's office and receive a certificate of his freedom.

3. No person was permitted to employ a Negro unless such Negro had the legal certificate attesting his freedom. A fine of from $10 to $50 was imposed for a failure to comply with this provision, one-half of which fine was to go to the informer and the other half to the state. An additional fine of 50 cents a day was imposed if the Negro employed or secreted was a fugitive slave.

4. Any person harboring or secreting a fugitive slave or preventing the lawful owner from retaking the same was subject to a fine of not less than $10 nor more than $50, one-half of which was to go to the informer and the other half to the state.

5. A Negro coming into the state with the required certificate must within two years record the same in the clerk's office in the county where he meant to reside and receive a certificate of such record.

6. Associate judges and justices of the peace were authorized and required to direct the sheriff or constable to arrest Negroes escaping into the state and deliver them to their masters.

7. Any person aiding a Negro without his certificate of freedom to move out of the state was subjected to a fine of $1,000, one-half of which was to go to the informer and the other half to the state.

On January 25, 1807, a supplemental act was passed providing:

1. That no Negro should be allowed to settle in Ohio unless within twenty days he gave a bond for $500 signed by two bondsmen as a guarantee of his good behavior and his ability to support himself.

2. That anyone harboring or concealing a fugitive slave should be fined $100, one-half to go to the informer and one-half to the overseers of the poor.

3. That no Negro should be allowed to give evidence in any case to which a white man was a party.

4. That the sixth section of the act of January 5, 1804, be repealed.

*Appendix VIII in Ph.D. diss. By James Harris Norton, "Quakers West of the Alleghenies and in Ohio to 1861, Western Reserve University, 1965.

Appendix C
Underground Railroad Routes

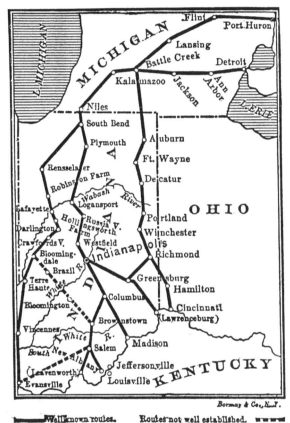

Bormay & Co., N.Y.

|━━━━━| Well known routes.   Routes not well established. |■ ■ ■ ■|

ROUTES THROUGH INDIANA AND MICHIGAN
IN 1848.

As traced by Lewis Falley.

From: The Underground Railroad From Slavery To Freedom
By Wilbur H. Siebert, as published in the series
The American Negro: His History and Literature.

Bibliography

Primary Sources

Birney, William. James G. *Birney and His Times*. D. Appleton and Company, 1890; reprint, New York: Negro Universities Press, 1969.

Coffin, Levi. *Reminiscences of Levi Coffin*. 3rd ed. Cincinnati: The Robert Clarke Company, 1898; reprint, New York: Arno Press and The New York Times, 1968.

Douglas, Frederick. *Life and Times of Frederick Douglass*. Hartford, Conn.: Park Publishing Company, 1881, reprint, Secaucus, N.J.: Citadel Press, 1983.

Dumond, Dwight, ed. *Letters of James Gillespie Birney*, 1831-1857. New York: D. Appleton-Century Co., 1938.

Ford, Henry A. and Ford, Mrs. Kate B., compilers. *History of Cincinnati, Ohio*. Cleveland: L.A.Williams & Co., 1881.

Haviland, Laura. *A Woman's Life-Work*. 3rd ed. 1883. reprint, Salem, New Hampshire: Ayer Company Publishers Inc., 1984.

Kraemer's Picturesque Cincinnati. Cincinnati: A.O. & G.A.Kraemer, 1898. reprint, Cincinnati: Ohio Book Store, 1985.

Moulton, Phillips P., ed. *The Journal and Major Essays of John Woolman*. New York: Oxford University Press, 1971.

Rosenblatt, Paul. *John Woolman*. New York: Twayne Publishing Co., 1969.

Siebert, Wilbur H. *The Underground Railroad-From Slavery to Freedom*. New York: The Macmillan Company, 1898. reprint, New York: Arno Press and *The New York Times*, 1968.

Still, William. *The Underground Railroad*. Philadelphia: Porter & Coates, 1872. reprint, Salem, New Hampshire: Ayer Company Publishers, Inc., 1968.

Secondary Sources

Barbour, Hugh, ed. *Slavery and Theology: Writings of Seven Quaker Reformers, 1800-1870.* Dublin, Indiana: Prinit Press, 1985.

Blockson, Charles L. *The Underground Railroad.* New York: Simon & Schuster, 1987.

Brandt, Nat. *The Town That Started the Civil War.* Syracuse: Syracuse University Press, 1990.

Campbell, Stanley W. *The Slave Catchers.* Chapel Hill, N.C.: The University of North Carolina Press, 1970.

Chaddock, Robert E. *Ohio Before 1850.* New York: AMS Press, Inc., 1967.

Cormany, Clayton Douglas. "Ohio's Abolitionist Campaign: A Study in the Rhetoric of Conversion." Ph.D. diss., Ohio State University, 1981.

Cosner, Shaaron. *The Underground Railroad.* New York: Franklin Watts, 1991.

Dudley, William, ed. *Slavery: Opposing Viewpoints.* San Diego: Greenhaven Press, Inc., 1992.

Fisher, Miles Mark. *Negro Slave Songs in the United States.* New York: Carol Publishing Group, 1990.

Fladeland, Betty. *James Gillespie Birney: Slaveholder to Abolitionist.* New York: Greenwood Press, 1955.

Gara, Larry. *Liberty Line: The Legend of the Underground Railroad.* Lexington, Ky.: University of Kentucky Press, 1961.

Hedrick, Joan D. *Harriet Beecher Stowe: A Life.* New York: Oxford University Press, 1994.

Hesseltine, William B. *A History of the South—1607-1936.* New York: Prentice-Hall, 1936.

Huff, Carolyn Barbara. "The Politics of Idealism: The Political Abolitionists of Ohio in Congress, 1840-1866." Ph.D. diss., University of North Carolina, 1970.

Kephart, Thomas J. *One Hundred Fifty Years of Cincinnati Monthly Meetings of Friends—1815-1965.* (Quaker Collection, Wilmington College, Wilmington, Ohio).

Lovell, Malcolm R., compiler. *Two Quaker Sisters (from the original diaries of Elizabeth Buffum Chace and Lucy Buffum Lovell).* New York: Liveright Publishing Corporation, 1937.

Norton, James Harris. "Quakers West of the Alleghenies and in Ohio to 1861." Ph.D. diss., Western Reserve University, 1965.

Norton, Thomas James. The Constitution of the United States: It's Sources and It's Application. New York: America's Future, Inc., 1941.

Nuermberger, Ruth Ketring. *The Free Produce Movement—A Quaker Protest Against Slavery.* Durham, North Carolina: Duke University Press, 1942.

Roseboom, Eugene H. *A History of the State of Ohio—The Civil War Era: 1850-1873.* Vol. IV, Columbus, Ohio: Ohio State Archaeological and Historical Society, 1944.

Soderlund, Jean R. *Quakers & Slavery: A Divided Spirit.* Princeton, N.J.: Princeton University Press, 1985.

Sprague, Stuart Seely, *The Autobiography of John P. Parker, Former Slave and Conductor on the Underground Railroad.* New York: W.W.Norton and Co., 1996.

Sterling, Dorothy. *Ahead of Her Time: Abby Kelley and The Politics of Antislavery.* New York: Norton and Co., 1991.

Time-Life Books. *African Americans: Voices of Triumph—Perseverance.* Alexandria, Va.: Time Life Inc., 1993.

Walls, Bryan E. *The Road That Led To Somewhere.* Windsor, Ontario: Olive Publishing Co., 1980.

Weeks, Stephen B. *Southern Quakers and Slavery.* New York: Bergman Publishers, 1968.

Weisenberger, Francis P. *A History of the State of Ohio—The Passing of the Frontier: 1825-1850.* Vol. III, Columbus, Ohio: Ohio State Archaeological and Historical Society, 1941.

Articles

Blockson, Charles L. "Escape from Slavery: The Underground Railroad." *National Geographic* (July 1984): 3-39.

Bruns, Roger. "Anthony Benezet's Assertion of Negro Equality." *Journal of Negro History*, (July 1971): 230-238.

Day, Blanch. "The Disquieting Quaker." *American Heritage* (April 1962): 102-103.

Holliday, Joseph E. "Freedmen's Aid Societies in Cincinnati, 1862-1870." *Bulletin of the Cincinnati Historical Society.* Vol. 22, (1964): 169-185.

Jennings, Judith. "The American Revolution and The Testimony of British Quakers Against the Slave Trade." *Quaker History* (Fall 1981): 99-103.

Jennings, Judith. "Mid-Eighteenth Century British Quakerism and the Response to the Problem of Slavery." *Quaker History* (Spring 1977): 23-40.

Lader, Lawrence. "Mad Old Man from Massachusetts." *American Heritage* (April 1961): 65-71.

Marable, Manning. "Death of the Quaker Slave Trade." *Quaker History* (Spring 1974): 17-33.

Siebert, Wilbur H. "A Quaker Section of the Underground Railroad in Northern Ohio." *Ohio Archaeological and Historical Quarterly.* (reprint 1930): 479-502.

Siebert, Wilbur H. "The Underground Railroad in Ohio" Ohio Archaeological and Historical Publications, Vol. 4. (1893, reprint 1993): 44-63.

Wax, Darold D. "Preferences For Slaves in Colonial America" *Journal of Negro History.* (October 1973): 371-401.

Westbury, Susan. "Slaves of Colonial Virginia: Where They Come From" *The William and Mary Quarterly.* (April 1985): 228-237.